T0209572

GOD
So Loved

What Do You See?

I See God's Love Everywhere!

Barbara J. Eaton

WESTBOW
P R E S S®
A DIVISION OF THOMAS NELSON
& ZONDERVAN

WestBow Press books may be ordered through booksellers or by contacting:

WestBow Press
A Division of Thomas Nelson & Zondervan
1663 Liberty Drive
Bloomington, IN 47403
www.westbowpress.com
1 (866) 928-1240

ISBN: 978-1-9736-5285-4 (sc)
ISBN: 978-1-9736-5286-1 (e)

Library of Congress Control Number: 2019901658

Print information available on the last page.

WestBow Press rev. date: 02/27/2019

For God so loved the world, that he gave his only begotten Son, that whosoever believeth in him should not perish, but have everlasting life.
—John 3:16 (King James Version)

CONTENTS

I give all the glory and praise to God Almighty who created the heaven and earth. I am thankful for God's amazing grace that made this book possible.

No one is an island unto himself or herself; we all need each other. I am so thankful to God for family and friends who prayed and gave support and encouragement to me while writing this book: my husband, Albert; daughter, Elaine; and friends Veronica Rogers, Daniel Driskell, Ann Brye, Al Stokes, Patricia Kennedy, and Dr. Hannah Hart. Thank you, all, for all you brought to this book. I could not have done it without your help. May the peace of God abide with you and your families forever.

PREFACE

This book is about the greatest love there ever was—Jesus, God's son, who left his home in glory and came to Earth to reconcile us back to the Father. Jesus is love.

The love He has for us is the same love He wants us to have for one another. It is not hard; just give your heart to Him, and the Holy Spirit will teach you how to love one another—the story of the Good Samaritan found in the tenth chapter of John is a fine example: A man was beaten and left for dead by the side of the road. A Samaritan came along and had compassion for him. He placed him on his beast and took him to an inn and cared for him. When he left, he told the innkeeper to take care of him until he returned. When he returned the next day, he paid the innkeeper for his services.

Just like the Samaritan, we too can be filled with compassion. All we have to do is let Jesus enter our hearts, forget our differences, focus on how much we are alike, and remember we are all God's creation.

INTRODUCTION

Colors are everywhere. Our world is a masterpiece, shaped and formed in the Master's hand. No human mind can stretch far enough to come up with the how, the why, the when, and the where. Some things are too high, wide, and deep for people to comprehend or understand fully. Some may wonder why God created us the way we are, with different colors of skin, hair, and eyes, speaking different languages, but I don't. Believing God is all wise and all-knowing reminds me of two scriptures. The first is from Deuteronomy 29:29: "The secret things belong unto the Lord our God, but those things which are revealed belong unto us and to our children forever, that we may do all the words of this law" (KJV).

The second is from the book of Job. Remember Job, a man from the land of Uz? He was called perfect and upright; he honored God. When he questioned God, God convinced Job of his ignorance and inability: "Where were you when I laid the foundations of the earth? Tell me, if you have understanding. Who determined its measurements? Surely you know! Or who stretched the line upon it? To what were its foundations fastened? Or who laid its cornerstone?" (Job 38:4–6 NKJV)

When God finished questioning him, Job replied, "I know that You can do everything" (Job 42:2 New King James Version).

God's creation is awesome. I feel we will all agree. His reason for the variety of colors I don't know. Just imagine if the only colors in the world were black, white, and gray. It would be a very dull and gloomy place to live.

I will not question God on the why. I am so glad God is a God of variety. The variety makes the world beautiful, our lives exciting and interesting. The only problem is some of us can't accept those who are different. Well, this book is not about the problems we have accepting each other, but about God's love for us and our ability to accept the fact that we are different. Yes, we're different in many ways but are alike in more ways than we would like to admit. But God knows the difference, and He is pleased with His creation.

Genesis 1:31 tells us, "And God saw every thing that he had made, and, behold, it was very good" (KJV). What do you see when you look at me through the eyes of Jesus? I see love looking at me. I see love looking at you.

REFLECTION

What do you see?

CHAPTER 1

In the Beginning

In the beginning God created the heaven and the earth. And the earth was without form, and void, and darkness was upon the face of the deep. And the Spirit of God moved upon the face of the waters.

—Genesis 1:1–2 (KJV)

God created the firmament, waters, dry land, and grass. He created the herb-yielding seeds and the fruit trees bearing fruit. He created the fowl of the air, the fish of the seas, the beasts of the earth, and the creeping creatures upon the earth. Then God said, "Let us make man." With His own hand, He created us out of the dust. God did not need permission from anyone concerning His creation. He spoke, and things came into existence. We are all His creation. Genesis 2:7 states, "And the Lord God formed man of the dust of the ground, and breathed into his nostrils the breath of life, and man became a living soul" (KJV).

After forming man, God placed him in a beautiful garden in Eden with wonderful colors everywhere on earth and in the heavens above us. This is more beautiful than our eyes can imagine: the green grass, blue sky and water; the red, black, white, and brown soil; snow-white clouds above us that turn shades of gray during storms; the trees with green and red leaves that turn gold, yellow, orange, and brown in the fall; the beautiful lilies of the field; and the rainbow after the rain. There are bright, brilliant colors everywhere for human eyes to see and enjoy.

What do you see looking at humankind? I see love. "For God so loved the world, He gave His only begotten son" (John 3:16 NKJV).

REFLECTION

God is a mighty God. He spoke, and creation came into existence.

CHAPTER 2

The Love of God

But the Lord said to Samuel, "Do not look at his appearance or at his physical stature, because I have refused him. For the Lord does not see as man sees; for man looks at the outward appearance but the Lord looks at the heart."

—1 Samuel 16:7 (NKJV)

God's love is like a river that flows freely. In the fourth chapter of John, we read of His love offered to a Samarian woman who was an outcast in her community. Jesus came to the well and asked her for a drink. He had no need of water, for He is living water.

How many times have we misjudged people because of who they are, how they look, their ethnic groups, and other differences? We must be careful because we may be entertaining angels.

The Samarian woman was blessed because she did not reject Jesus's love. She drank of the living water and then ran and told others about Jesus of Nazareth: "Come see a man" (John 4:29 NKJV).

The love of God is so powerful that it softens even hearts of stone and opens even blind eyes.

Those who are blessed to see with physical eyes can see colors and appreciate the beauty of God's world. Unfortunately, there are those who can see with physical eyes but are unable to see with spiritual eyes. They are unable to see the love Christ has for each of us. Because of the love within, some who are without physical sight are able to see and feel more of God's beauty around them and in their fellow human. The love shown to others from those who have no sight is sometimes greater than those who see with physical eyes.

Love is a heart thing; it comes from Jesus, who gave His life for us on Calvary. What held Jesus on the cross? Was it the nails? Was it the soldiers? It was His love.

The love of Jesus is the substance that's holding the world together. It keeps the sun in the sky, the moon and stars shining, the cool breeze blowing on a hot summer day, the rain falling from the sky to give continued life to the earth and the seas and oceans in their banks. I could go on forever. Oh, what power it is in the love of Jesus! Listen to the sounds of the earth and the music in the air. Everything gives praise to God the creator. Humankind, who are we? Scripture says we are made a little lower than the angels. We were created because of God's love. "And God saw every thing that he had made, and, behold, it was very good" (Genesis 1:31 KJV).

Why can't we see the beauty of God's creation? Diversity is what He wanted. All through creation, He was very pleased. Our diversity did not come by chance. This was and is God's will. God so loved the world. How much is *so*? God loves us so. How high is so, how low is so, and how wide is so? No one knows. God so loved us that He gave His only Son. Who do you know who would give his or her only son to save you? I don't know of anyone but God, our heavenly Father.

What do you see when you look at me through the eyes of Jesus? I see love looking at me. I see love looking at you.

REFLECTION

Jesus offers us living water.

CHAPTER 3

God's Amazing Love

And hope maketh not ashamed, because the love of God is shed abroad in our hearts by the Holy Ghost which is given unto us.

—Romans 5:5 (KJV)

Yes, everything has color, even humans. God made us with different colors of skin: red, yellow, black, white, or brown. We also have different cultures and ways of doing things, and different languages, but we are alike in more ways than we are different. What do you see? A mother with two or more children sees each of her children differently. They look, act, and sound different. However, her love for them is the same because they are children of God, just as we are children of God. "For God so loved the world that he gave his only son." That's love.

Those who believe in God, Jehovah, Jesus, and the Son of God believe He was crucified on Calvary's cross and rose from the dead for our sins. Those are the ones who are led and comforted by the Holy Spirit, the ones who are waiting for the second coming of the Lamb of God. The ones who see love when looking at others. Romans 5:5 says it plainly: "And hope maketh not ashamed, because the love of God is shed abroad in our hearts by the Holy Ghost which is given unto us."

God's amazing love has been given to us through the Holy Spirit. It is left to us to nourish it by daily Bible reading and prayer. The warm glow of His unconditional love will radiate within us, anointing us to look at each other through the eyes of love. Jesus tells us in Matthew 5:44–45:

> Love your enemies, bless them that curse you, do
> good to them that hate you, and pray for them

which despitefully use you, and persecute you; that ye may be the children of your Father which is in heaven; for He maketh his sun to rise on the evil and on the good, and sendeth rain on the just and on the unjust. (KJV)

Who can describe God? His love for us can't be measured. He loves us unconditionally. He is the Good Shepherd.

In the parable of the lost sheep, the shepherd left the ninety-nine to go find the one that was lost. This parable shows us that we are all precious to Him. He has no favorite. We can't understand His love for us or His plan for our lives, but we can trust Him.

We find in the second chapter of Joshua a woman named Rahab. She was a sinful woman, but God used her to help the two men who were sent to spy on the land of Jericho. Rahab hid the spies and helped them escape. Because of her faith and courage, she was used in God's plan for the children of Israel. Her action led to her name being recorded in "the book of genealogy of Jesus Christ, the son of David, the son of Abraham" (Matthew 1:1 NKJV).

All through the Bible, God shows us there are differences in us. Even though we are different, God neither shows nor sees any differences in His children. This is His amazing love given to all.

"For God so loved the world, that he gave his only begotten Son, that whosoever believeth on him should not perish, but have everlasting life. John 3:16 (KJV) What held Jesus on Calvary's cross? God's amazing love.

Pray that your heart will be filled with love for Jesus and for your neighbor so that your thoughts, words, and actions will be motivated by the love that is from Jesus. Then and only then will you be able to love your neighbor as you love yourself. What do you see when you look at me?

REFLECTION

What do you see?

CHAPTER 4

Self-Examination: What Do You See?

*If a man say, I love God and hateth his brother, he is
a liar; for he that loveth not his brother whom he hath
seen, how can he love God whom he hath not seen?*

—1 John 4:20 (KJV)

How important are self-examinations? If you ask this question, you may get different answers. There are times when self-examinations in some medical conditions have saved and even prolonged lives. Some health conditions have been detected early because of one's self-examination. But there are more reasons why self-examinations are important.

Self-examination of one's appearance is important to most of us. We will all agree that the invention of the mirror is an appreciated item. We inspect ourselves before going out into public and make necessary changes if needed.

But there are times when we place too much emphasis on our outer appearance and not enough on the inner being, our heart. 1 Samuel 16:7 says, "The Lord said unto Samuel, 'Look not on his countenance, or on the height of his stature; because I have refused him: for the Lord seeth not as man seeth; for man looketh on the outward appearance, but the Lord looketh on the heart'" (KJV).

Personal examinations help us to be careful how we look at and judge our brothers and sisters. Matthew 7:3 says, "And why do you look at the speck in your brother's eye, but do not consider the plank in your own eye?" (NKJV)

God said it is not good for man to be alone. We need each other. When disasters strike or when we are placed in a situation where we have no control and can't help ourselves, we look to others for help. It is at these times that we pull together and forget our differences.

It doesn't matter what the religious preference, financial status, educational background, neighborhood we live in, or the color of one's skin. It is at these times that the love Jesus planted in each of us is shared. All our differences are forgotten. There is almost always a helping hand reaching out to you in times of trouble.

Yes, there may be differences, but we need each other on this life's journey. God so loved the world. That is why we should love one another, because He loves us so. What do you see in your self-examination—good or bad? I see love looking at you when looking at you through the eyes of Jesus.

Therefore, who are we to judge one another? When Jesus looked down on the people at the bottom of the cross, He said, "Father, forgive them, for they do not know what they do" (Luke 23:34 NKJV). He is still looking down on us with that same forgiveness and love. Jesus loves us, and He gave His life for us. Now He is asking us to love the Lord our God with all our heart and our neighbors as we do ourselves.

REFLECTION

We are all blind until we accept Jesus.
What do you see?

CHAPTER 5

What Do We Gain?

And I John saw the holy city, new Jerusalem, coming down from God out of heaven, prepared as a bride adorned for her husband. And I heard a great voice out of heaven saying, Behold, the tabernacle of God is with man, and he will dwell with them, and they shall be his people, and God himself shall be with them, and be their God. And God shall wipe away all tears from their eyes; and there shall be no more death, neither sorrow, nor crying, neither shall there be any more pain; for the former things are passed away.

—Revelation 21:2–4 (KJV)

On that great day, when Jesus, the Lamb of God, will be crowned King of kings and Lord of lords, all God's children, Jews and Gentiles, shall come together. People of all races shall lift their voices in praise, hallelujah to the Lamb of God.

John wrote in Revelation 21:3–5, "And I heard a great voice out of heaven saying, Behold, the tabernacle of God is with men, and he will dwell with them, and they shall be his people, and God himself shall be with them and be their God. And God shall wipe away all tears from their eyes; and there shall be no more death, neither sorrow, nor crying, neither shall there be any more pain; for the former things are passed away. And he that sat upon the throne said, Behold, I make all things new. And he said unto me, 'Write; for these words are true and faithful'" (KJV).

Jesus is love, and this is how we know He lives within us—when we love one another.

John tells us in John 15:12, "This is my commandment, that you love one another, as I have loved you" (NKJV). Also, in John 3:16, "For God so loved the world that He gave His only begotten Son, that whoever believes, in Him should not perish but have everlasting life" (NKJV). What do we gain?

What do you see when you look at me? What do I see when I look at you through the eyes of Jesus? I see love looking at me, I see love looking at you.

We all are looking, but what do we see? Look in the mirror at yourself and say, God so loves me; therefore, I can love myself and others." God's love has been poured into our hearts through the Holy Spirit. What do we gain by loving Jesus and one another? We gain eternal life. Christ's death and resurrection give us hope and assurance of a new life with Him. A life that will never end and where only love, joy, and peace abide.

"WHAT DO WE GAIN?"

B.J. Eaton

Why are you looking
at me so strange?
I am just a clump of dirt
just like you,
that the Master gave grace
and breathed into me the breath of life.
Why are you looking
at me so strange?
We are both the same,
struggling through this life,
hoping for heaven's gain.
Think about it: what do we gain
when we mistreat each other?
I tell you
there is nothing gained.
We lose a piece of ourselves,
because we are all
shaped from the same dirt
in the Master's hand.

REFLECTION

What do we lose?

AFTERWORD

As a new writer, I have found that when God gives me something to write, it is for me first and then for others.

While writing this book, I was sitting in a doctor's office waiting for my mother. I looked around at the people in the room. I was reminded that I was looking at children of God. Good or bad, kind or not so kind, black, white, yellow, red, or brown, they were His children and He loves them. The song "God So Loved" came to my mind. If I could look through the eyes of Jesus, what would I see? In my heart, I knew I would see love looking at each of us because Jesus is love.

"For God so loved the world, that he gave His only begotten Son, that whosoever believeth in him should not perish, but have everlasting life" (John 3:16 KJV).

It is my prayer that readers will feel the love of God as they read this book in its entirety. Paul tells us in Roman 8:38–39, "For I am persuaded that neither death nor life, nor angels not principalities nor powers, nor things present nor things to come, nor height nor depth, nor any other created thing, shall be able to separate us from the love of God which is Christ Jesus our Lord" (NKJV). God's love is *awesome*!

Let us obey Him: "For this is my commandment that you love one another as I love you." John 15:12 (KJV)

Red, yellow, black, white, or brown the color of your skin, rich or poor, physical status, it does not matter. God loves you just the way you are. You are made in His image. It is the heart that God our father is looking at in us. What He sees there is important. What do you see when you look at me through the eyes of Jesus? I see love looking at me; I see love looking at you. Jesus is love. If we truly love God, we will love our sisters and brothers, who we see daily.

Look again at 1 John 4:20. "If a man say, I love God and hateth his brother, he is a liar for he that loveth not his brother whom he hath seen, how can he love God whom he hath not seen?" (KJV)

What do you see?

God is our creator who loves us. His plan for us from the beginning was done all in love. None of us can question or explain His love for us. We can only say, "God so loved." Who among us would give our only son to save man from his sin? God did, for you and me. Our sins were so egregious that His father could not stand to look on Him as He hanged on the cross.

Let everyone examine himself or herself and see why we can't love our brothers and sisters we see every day. Is Jesus in us, as we proclaim? The Holy Spirit is knocking at our hearts. Open the door and feel the love of Jesus.

On July 8, 2018, my pastor ended his sermon with a story he heard. "A little boy was very sick and needed heart surgery. The doctor talked with the boy and his mother about the operation. He told the boy he would go into his heart and fix it. The little boy told the doctor, "When you open my heart you will see Jesus. My Sunday school teacher told me Jesus lives in my heart."

Several days after surgery the doctor talked with the mother and boy. He told them the surgery was a success. The boy would make a full recovery. The little boy looked at the doctor and asked, "What did you find in my heart?" With tears running down his cheek, the doctor said, "I found Jesus."

This is what happens when we share the love of Jesus. If we love the Lord our God with all our hearts, souls, and minds, and our neighbors as ourselves, the world would change. It would be a better place for us to live if Jesus lived in our hearts. Red, yellow, black, white, or brown, God so loves us, and He commands that we love one another to be his disciple. *It's all about forgiveness and love.*

LET US PRAY:

"Our Father in heaven, Hallowed be Your name. Your kingdom come. Your will be done On earth as it is in heaven. Give us this day our daily bread. And forgive us our debts, as we forgive our debtors. And do not lead us into temptation, But deliver us from the evil one. For Yours is the kingdom and the power and the glory forever. Amen" (Matthew 6:9–13 NKJV).

THE WORDS OF THE SONG "GOD SO LOVED"

What do you see when you look at me through the eyes of Jesus? I see love looking at me. Red, yellow, black, white and brown, we are all God's creation; all that He made He said was good.

"For this is my commandment, that you love one another as I have loved you." John 1

Jesus is love, Jesus is love, God so loved the world He gave His only son. What do you see when you look at me through the eyes of Jesus? I see love looking at me, I see love looking at you.

REFLECTION

What's in my heart?

ABOUT THE AUTHOR

Barbara J. Eaton early years were spent on a farm with her grandparents. They were poor farmers. Even though the times were hard, her grandparents shared what they had with their neighbors and their neighbors shared with them. There, she received love and was taught Christian values.

This rural community was an example of God's love. The community was made up of black, Indian, and white families. They worked, played, and shared what they had to make life better during these hard times. Living in this community taught her so much about God's love.

Barbara worked for thirty-two years as a secretary. After retiring, she decided to take piano lessons. She was brought up as a child singing in the church choir and had a love of music. Her parents could not afford a piano, nor could they afford lessons. It was a great challenge for her to learn to play the piano as an adult. She was taught as a child, "Nothing beats a try." She tried—and she is now playing for her church school and community outreach.

As a young woman, she dreamed of one day writing a book. She never dreamed she would be the author of two books. In 2009, led by the Holy Spirit, she wrote her first song, "To Hear from God" which led her to write a book about traditional gospel music. She was inspired by God again to write this second book, "God So Loved."

God So Loved

Barbara J. Eaton
Arr. Daniel G. Driskell

God So Loved

love   Je - sus is love___   God   so   loved   the

world   that   He   gave___   His   on - ly   son.

1, 2.   3.

Printed in the United States
By Bookmasters